TOM THUMB

TOM THUMB

RETOLD AND ILLUSTRATED BY

RICHARD JESSE WATSON

HARCOURT BRACE JOVANOVICH, Publishers

San Diego   New York   London

HBJ

Copyright © 1989 by Richard Jesse Watson

Requests for permission to make copies of any
part of this work should be mailed to:
Permissions Department,
Harcourt Brace Jovanovich, Publishers, 8th Floor,
Orlando, Florida 32887.

Library of Congress Cataloging-in-Publication Data
Watson, Richard Jesse.
Tom Thumb.
Summary: After many adventures, a tiny boy, no
bigger than his father's thumb, earns a place as the
smallest Knight of the Round Table.
[1. Fairy tales. 2. Folklore] I. Title.
PZ8.W334T0 1989   398.2′1′0943   [E]   87-12045
ISBN 0-15-289280-X
ISBN 0-15-289281-8 (pbk.)

B C D E F
A B C D E (pbk.)

Printed in Hong Kong

The illustrations in this book were done in egg tempera
and watercolor on Strathmore illustration board.
The display type was hand-lettered by
Connie Gustafson Smiley.
The text type was set in ITC Berkeley Old Style
by Thompson Type, San Diego, California.
Printed and bound by South China Printing Co. Ltd.,
Hong Kong
Production supervision by Warren Wallerstein
and Rebecca Miller
Designed by Joy Chu

For Rebecca Sue, my love

And thank you, Benjamin,
for being a splendid Tom

ong ago, in the days of knights and giants, wizards and
færies, there lived a poor farmer and his wife.

One day a beggar came to their humble cottage. Though they had
little, the farmer and his wife were kind to everyone, and they gave the
poor old man a big bowl full of fresh goat's milk and some coarse brown
bread. As it happened, the beggar was none other than Merlin—the
greatest of all wizards—traveling in disguise. And Merlin took the
couple's kindness to heart.

Wise Merlin noticed that although everything was neat and
comfortable in the cottage, the farmer and his wife seemed sad. He asked
them the cause of their sorrow. They told him it was because they had
no children.

"I long for a child," the tearful wife declared, "even if the babe were
no bigger than my husband's thumb."

The next day Merlin set out to visit the queen of færies. The idea of such a wee little child had tickled his fancy.

And in due season the farmer and his wife were blessed with the tiniest of tiny boys. The færies named him Tom Thumb and dressed him in clothes only færies could have made: an oak leaf for a hat, a tunic spun of spiderweb, and a jacket woven from thistledown. His breeches were of the smoothest feathers, and his stockings were shaped from apple rind tied with eyelashes from his mother's eyes. His shoes were of mouse skin, with the soft fur on the inside.

Tom grew older, but he never grew bigger. He was a clever lad, full of jokes and games, and he loved to explore. But because he was so small his curiosity could be very dangerous.

One day his mother was making a cake, and Tom was curious to see how it was made. He climbed up to the edge of the mixing bowl. But his foot slipped and he plumped right into the batter, unseen by his mother who poured the batter into the cake pan and pushed the pan into the oven!

Tom's mouth was so filled with batter that he could not cry out. But as he felt the batter getting hotter, he kicked and struggled violently. The half-baked cake made such a noise wiggling and jiggling in the oven that his mother thought it was bewitched, and she flung it out the door.

A poor peddler passing by picked up the pan and started to tuck it into his bundle. But Tom had cleared his throat and begun to holler. The peddler dropped the pan and ran screaming down the road. Tom squirmed free and made his way home, where his mother washed him in a teacup bath and tucked him into bed.

The next day Tom's mother tried to keep him at her side at all times, even when it was time to milk the cow in the meadow. Since the wind was strong and she feared he might be blown away, she tied poor Tom to a thistlehead with one of her long hairs. Thinking this looked like a tasty morsel, the cow curled her tongue around the thistle and Tom Thumb both.

So there he was, dodging cow teeth and roaring, "Mother! Help!" as loud as a thumb-sized lad can roar.

Before Tom's mother could even figure out where he was, the cow heard the awful noise in her throat and coughed Tom up. His mother caught him in her apron and carried him home, safe once more.

It seemed that every day brought new perils for Tom. This worried his poor parents, for they loved him dearly. Tom was sorry to add to their hardships and often wished he could be useful to his parents and help to ease their lives.

Tom was thinking about this very problem one fine morning as he went with his father to drive the cattle home.

As he was hopping and scrambling to keep up with his father, a raven flying overhead mistook Tom for a frog, and swooped down and carried him off.

They flew north over the forest to a seaside cliff. The raven, discovering at last that Tom was not a fat and tasty frog, dropped him on the battlements of a dark castle.

It was the castle, Tom quickly learned, of a giant named Grumbong. Because giants can't think very well they can be dangerous when they get in a bad mood. But this giant never bothered anyone. The færies had given him a special charm to calm him—a seashell he could put to his ear to hear the soothing sound of the ocean. No one knew the secret of the shell except the færies, but Tom watched the giant and figured it out for himself. He felt safe, and he called out as loud as he could when Grumbong came near.

Too late Tom remembered that although giants are brave they are easily startled. Indeed, when the giant saw tiny Tom, he threw up his arms, accidentally breaking the string that held his shell, which fell to the ground and broke into pieces. Grumbong turned on Tom. Before Tom knew what was happening, the giant had picked him up, tossed him into his mouth, and swallowed him!

This was Tom's worst peril yet. He kicked and struggled in the giant's insides with a frenzy. Minutes later, Grumbong turned green and squeamy and spit the boy out over the end of the battlement and into the sea.

This surely would have been the end of Tom Thumb had not a big fish, thinking him a shrimp, rushed at him and gulped him down.

Tom had a lot of time to think in the fish's belly, and he said to himself, "No one is going to eat me again—ever!" He found a sturdy fishbone and made himself a sword, so that creatures would think twice before swallowing him.

Days passed, and at last the fish was caught by a fisherman who was the royal fisherman to the great King Arthur.

Imagine the surprise of the servants and scullions when they cut the fine fish open and found Tom inside! They took him at once to the king, who was delighted with the tiny lad.

Things went well for Tom at first. With his quips and games, he amused the king and queen, as well as all the knights and ladies of the court.

But one day, as Tom was playing in the courtyard, he saw the court cook, who was always in a hurry. The cook nearly stepped on Tom, who cried, "Don't squash me!"

Alarmed, the cook slipped, dropped the dessert he had just made for the king, and fell face first into it. The cook flew into a rage and went straight to the king: "Tom has ruined your favorite dessert on purpose!"

The king believed the angry cook and had Tom imprisoned in a mousetrap.

Lonely days passed, and Tom sighed aloud, "What will become of my poor parents? What will become of me—will they cut off my head?"

"Not for a while," came the voice of a friendly mouse. "King Arthur and all the Knights of the Round Table have gone to battle. The giant Grumbong is waging war against the castle for no reason."

"I know why!" gasped Tom. "It's because Grumbong's special charm has been broken. Nothing will calm him but that. We must get him another."

With the help of the castle mice, Tom escaped from his prison. He led them to the nearby shore, where they found the largest shell on the beach. With the aid of some rabbits and squirrels who carried the shell, Tom raced ahead on the swiftest mouse and led them all to the battlefield.

They arrived at a fierce and horrible scene. The giant Grumbong heaved boulders and ripped up trees. The knights were ready to stop the giant with their lances, arrows, and broadswords.

Tom felt useless. He didn't know how to get the shell to the giant without being trod upon by horses, cut asunder by flailing swords, or mashed by Grumbong's stamping feet.

Finally, he took his tiny fishbone sword and poked a small hole in one end of the shell. Then Tom and all the animals together blew into it as hard as they could.

The sound that came from the shell was deafening. All fighting on the battlefield stopped, and everyone turned and stared. In the silence, Tom on his mousey steed led the shell-bearing animals straight up to the feet of the towering giant.

As soon as he saw the shell, Grumbong carefully picked it up and put it to his ear. A smile came to his face and he said, "Good shell. Nice ocean, pretty sound." Then he turned and went back to his castle, quiet and content again.

The king was so grateful to Tom for ending the battle that he made Tom a knight—Sir Thomas Thumb— and offered him all the gold he wanted, to take back to his parents.

Even a single coin was too much for Tom to carry, so the court carpenters built tiny wagons to carry his prize. Pulling the wagons were rabbits and squirrels and cats and mice, with an honor guard of the king's favorite dogs. Tom came last, riding on his mouse—a sight that brought laughter and cheers from the people as the procession marched home with Tom's treasures.

And so it was that Tom Thumb, in the end, helped his parents and earned his place as the smallest Knight of the Round Table.

THE END

Richard Jesse Watson has worked as a farmhand, welder, carpet layer, letter carrier, and graphic designer, as well as an artist. His love of art and literature began when he was a child, and he cannot remember a time when he was not drawing and writing. After studying art at Pasadena City College and the Art Center College of Design, he was an assistant art director for World Vision International and an artist for Hallmark Cards. He is the illustrator of *Bronwen, the Traw, and the Shape Shifter* by James Dickey (HBJ, 1986), a *Parents' Choice* Award winner for Illustration, and more recently, *The High Rise Glorious Skittle Skat Roarious Sky Pie Angel Food Cake* by Nancy Willard (HBJ, 1990), an IRA-CBC Children's Choice that *The New York Times Book Review* deemed "enchanting and inspiring." Richard Watson was named Ezra Jack Keats Fellow of 1987 by the Kerlan Collection of the University of Minnesota.

He lives with his wife, Susi, and their three children in Port Townsend, Washington.